The Very Last First

Jaap Tuinman

CONSULTANTS
Anna Cresswell
Gail Heald-Taylor
Lynda Hodson
Glen Huser

ADVISER
Moira McKenzie

PROGRAMME EDITOR
Kathleen Doyle

Schofield & Sims Ltd
Educational Publishers

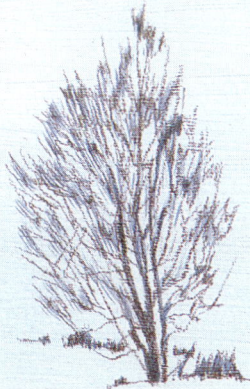

Journeys

Level Seven
The Very Last First

TEACHER CONTRIBUTORS
Bev Bishoff
Marion Yarema

ISBN 0-7217-0581-2

Printed and bound in England
ABCDEFGHIJ 9876543210

First printed 1985

ART/DESIGN CONSULTANT
Hugh Michaelson

TYPESETTING
PFB Art & Type Ltd.
FILM
Colourgraph Reproduction
Systems Inc.
PRINTING
Chorley & Pickersgill Ltd.

ACKNOWLEDGEMENTS

For kind permission to reprint copyrighted material, acknowledgement is hereby made to the following:

Jan Andrews for her story "The Very Last First". Reprinted by permission of the author.

Mary Blount Christian for her story "Nothing Much Happened Today". Reprinted with the permission of the author.

Crabtree Publishing Company for "A Long School Day" from *Early Schools* by Bobbie Kalman. Copyright © 1982 Crabtree Publishing Company Ltd., Toronto.

Doubleday & Company, Inc. for the poem "General Store" from *Taxis and Toadstools*. Copyright © 1926 by Rachel Field. Reprinted by permission of Doubleday & Company, Inc. Also for excerpts from *Mime: A Playbook of Silent Fantasy*. Copyright © 1978 by Kay Hamblin.

Fiddlehead, Winter 1964 for "A Child's Winter Song" by Sylvia Osterbind.

Harper & Row, Publishers, Inc. for the verse from the poem on page 23 of *Near the Window Tree, Poems and Notes*, by Karla Kuskin, 1975.

The Horn Book, Inc. for "The Woodcutter's Hunh-Sayer: A Nasreddin Hodja Story", reprinted from *The Horn Book Magazine* (February 1964).

Mrs. S. R. Guttormsson for the excerpts from *Ian of Red River* by R. Guttormsson. Reprinted by permission.

Kids Can Press for the adaptation of "The Little Rooster's Diamond Penny" by Marina McDougall. Reprinted by permission of Kids Can Press, Toronto. Story copyright © 1978 by Marina McDougall.

Little, Brown & Co. for the excerpts from *The Book of Think* by Marilyn Burns. Copyright © 1976 by the Yolla Bolly Press. A Brown Paper School Book.

Scholastic Press for the poem "No Picture" from *Arm in Arm*. Copyright © 1969 by Remy Charlip.

The Scrimshaw Press for the adaptation of "The Raven, the Dove and the Whale" by Kimberly Buis, age 9, from *There's a Sound in the Sea*.

Viking Penguin Inc. for a selection from *Journey Cake, Ho!* by Ruth Sawyer and Robert McCloskey. Copyright © 1953 by Ruth Sawyer. Copyright © renewed 1981 by David Durand and Robert McCloskey. Reprinted by permission of Viking Penguin Inc. Also for "Wales's Tale" by Susan Saunders. Copyright © 1980 by Susan Saunders.

Virgo Press for the excerpt from "Letter to Vietnam" from the film by Eugene Buia.

Every reasonable precaution has been taken to trace the owners of copyrighted material and to make due acknowledgement. Any omission will be gladly rectified in future editions.

Contents

ALL ABOUT NOTHING		7
Nothing Much Happened Today	Story	9
No Picture	Poem	14
Can You Imagine That!	Article	15
Wales's Tale	Story	19
It's All in Your Head	Article	27

FIRST ADVENTURES — 31

The Gift	Story	32
General Store	Poem	36
A Long School Day	Article	37
Canada Is My Home	Article	43
A Winter Song	Poem	47
The Very Last First	Story	48

THE TALE SPINNERS — 54

A Tale of the Hodja	Folk tale	56
The Little Rooster's Diamond Penny	Folk tale	59
Meet the Author	Interview	66
The Raven, the Dove and the Whale	Story	70
Journey Cake, Ho!	Folk tale	73

All about Nothing

You're in your room.
You're playing with your best friend
or your brother or sister and all of
a sudden, there's a loud crash in
the room—BOOM-BAM. It sounds
like the whole world caved in
your room and your mum yells up,
"What are you doing up there?"
"Nothing. We're doing nothing."

By Bob Schneider

7

Nothing Much Happened Today

By Mary Blount Christian
Illustrated by Sarie Jenkins

Mrs. Maeberry held her groceries tightly. She ran home to tell her children about seeing the police chase a robber. But when she turned down her street, her mouth flew open. Soap bubbles—hundreds, thousands, maybe millions of soap bubbles—were drifting from her front window. She ran inside the house shouting, "What happened? What happened here?"

Stephen shrugged. "Nothing much, really."

"But the bubbles?" she yelled. "Look at those bubbles!"

Stephen shrugged again. His sister Elizabeth mumbled, "Maybe we did use too many soapsuds when we gave Popsicle a bath."

"The dog? You bathed the dog?" Mrs. Maeberry asked. "Why did you bath the dog?"

"He got sugar stuck all over his fur," Alan, the youngest, said.

Mrs. Maeberry set her groceries down. "I was gone five minutes, just five minutes. How could Popsicle get sugar in his fur?"

"He got sugar in his fur when he knocked over the sugar tin. That was when he was chasing the cat through the kitchen," Stephen added.

Mrs. Maeberry gasped. "Cat? We haven't got a cat."

"I guess you could say it was a visiting cat," Stephen explained. "It came through the window."

"The window?" his mother exclaimed. "That cat broke the glass?"

Stephen shook his head. "No. The window was open. We had to let the smoke out."

Mrs. Maeberry gasped. "Smoke? What smoke?"

"The smoke from the oven when the cake mixture spilled over," Elizabeth volunteered.

Mrs. Maeberry waved her arms. "Why were you baking a cake?"

"For the school cake stall," Alan reminded her.

"But," his mother protested, "I baked that before I went to the shop."

"We know," Stephen said, "but that one got ruined."

"Ruined?" his mother repeated. "How could my beautiful cake get ruined? I was gone ten minutes, only ten minutes."

"The cake was knocked on to the floor, and it's a good thing it was too," Elizabeth said.

"I don't understand this at all," Mrs. Maeberry said.

"It's not so bad," Stephen said. "We used too many soapsuds on Popsicle because he was covered with sugar. He knocked the sugar over chasing the cat. The cat came through the window when we let out the smoke. The smoke is from the spilled cake mixture in the oven. We were replacing the cake you baked because that one got knocked off by the policeman."

Mrs. Maeberry's eyebrows shot up. "Policeman! What policeman?"

"The policeman that ran in after the robber," Alan told her.

"MY robber?" his mother gasped. "I—I mean the grocery robber?" She sank into a chair. "But tell me, please. Tell me how a robber and a policeman ruined my cake."

Stephen smiled. "That's easy. The policeman was chasing the robber around our kitchen table. Then the policeman accidentally knocked the cake down on the floor. The robber skidded in the icing."

Elizabeth interrupted. "And when the robber fell, he hit his head on Alan's head. And you know how hard Alan's head is."

"I know. I know," her mother said. "Let me see now. The robber ran into here and the policeman chased him. They ruined the cake. When you baked a new one, you made the oven smoky. Then you opened the window to let the smoke out and the cat came in. Popsicle chased the cat and knocked the sugar tin on himself. And that's when you bathed him with too many soapsuds?"

"That's right," the three of them said together. "And that's when you came home."

Mrs. Maeberry said, "I *know* I couldn't have been gone very long. Not very long at all."

"We *told* you nothing much happened today," Stephen said. "How was your day?"

"Nothing much," his mother said, sliding further into the chair. "Nothing much."

No Picture

By Remy Charlip

NO WORM
NO BIRD
NO CAT
NO DOG
NO MAN
NO HOUSE
NO TREE
NO WOODS
NO LAND
NO WATER
NO CLOUDS
NO SKY
NO SUN
NOTHING

NO PICTURE

14

Can You Imagine That!

Photographed by Harold Whyte

Some people believe there's something when there's nothing. That's the art of mime.

Put yourself in neutral

A mime artist always starts from neutral: feet slightly apart, knees bent a little, back straight. Stand comfortably, then relax your face and let your eyes look at nothing. If you start to smile or move, shift back to neutral.

Speaking with your body

The artist uses the body to bring the audience's imagination to life. Without words, the artist must "create" the object for the audience to "see".

If you wanted to "create" a ball, how would you do it?

Picture a ball hanging in space before you

Approach it with a flat hand. Connect with the surface. Snap your hand into a curve. Discover the shape in your palm and with your fingers.

Feel the texture of the ball. Slide your fingers over it. Change the texture. Ripple your fingers over a bumpy surface. Squeeze a spongy ball.

Snap your other hand into a curve on the opposite side of the ball. The curves mirror each other. Tense your hands around the shape.

Explore the ball shape. Hold it by the sides, by the top and bottom. Balance it in one hand. Lift your elbows and let your arms move with it.

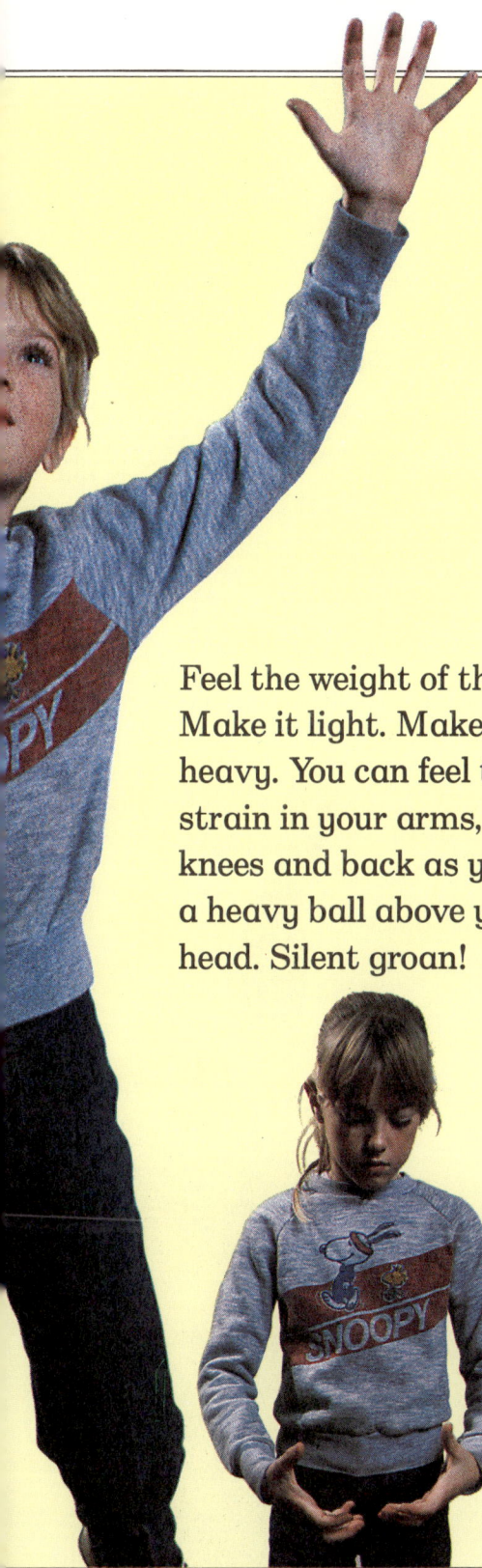

Feel the weight of the ball. Make it light. Make it heavy. You can feel the strain in your arms, bended knees and back as you lift a heavy ball above your head. Silent groan!

How to catch a big nothing

Toss the ball into the air. Your hand snaps flat as the ball leaves your palm. Follow it up and down with your eyes and head. Your waiting palm is stretched flat.
Emphasize the catch as: 1) your palm and fingers snap into the curve of the ball; 2) your hand snaps slightly downward with the weight; 3) your head snaps and stops abruptly as the ball comes to rest. These movements will be harder to see when the ball is light, but even a ping-pong ball gets the "snap" treatment.

Repeat tossing and catching many kinds of balls, using one hand or both hands.

Teaming up on nothing

Toss a ball to someone. Your eyes and head show where it's going. Both players' heads snap to emphasize the catch.

Roll the ball to someone. Let your whole body glide to describe the rolling.

Bounce a ball to someone. Together, follow the bounce with your head and eyes.

Play team games like volley-ball, netball or rounders. Score goals at soccer. Hit runs at cricket. To keep all eyes on one ball is really the game here.

What else can you "create" from nothing? In mime, the only limit is your—and your audience's—imagination.

18

Wales's Tale

By Susan Saunders
Illustrated by Tina Holdcroft

It was market day and Sara had vegetables to sell. She packed everything into two large baskets. Then she tied both baskets to her bicycle and rode into town.

The market was crowded and noisy. It was so noisy that Sara didn't hear the donkey at first.

"Pardon me," the donkey said. Then, "Pardon me," he said louder.

"Oh!" Sara cried with a start.

"I'm in terrible trouble," the donkey began, "and you have such a kind face. Will you help me?"

"What must I do?" Sara asked.

"I am not what I seem," the donkey explained. "My name is Wales and usually I am a handsome prince."

"Prince of what?" Sara asked.

"A kingdom beyond the mountains," Wales said. "A magician turned me into a donkey. Will you help me?"

But Sara had vegetables to sell, and her lettuce was wilting in the hot sun. "I will have to sell my vegetables first," she said.

"I'll do that for you," Wales offered. "Crisp cucumbers," he called. "Toothsome tomatoes. Ravishing radishes."

Everyone came to see the talking donkey, and Sara's vegetables sold quickly at very good prices.

19

"*Now* will you help me?" the donkey asked.

"Certainly," Sara replied. "What's fair is fair."

"Good," Wales said. "First, we must find a good wizard who can tell us how to remove this spell."

Sara thought. "I don't know any wizards," she said, "but there is a fortune-teller."

"That will have to do," Wales replied, and he trotted beside Sara to a pink house at the edge of town.

Madame Mira was outside. "I specialize in love potions," she told them. "I've never been called upon to transform anyone. But I do have some things in the tool shed that might be useful."

Madame Mira pulled out an old notebook: "Calming storms... charms for the plough..." She paused. "Here it is: Spells for transformation. Princes into toads. No, toads into princes." Madame Mira sighed. "I'm afraid that's as close as I can get."

"I'll try it," said Wales.

Madame Mira copied the directions on to a scrap of paper and handed it to Sara. "That will be seventy-eight pence."

"It's a poem," said Sara, and she read it to Wales as they walked back to her bicycle.

*"From toad to prince
without a care—
add white to pink
and leave it there.
Then yellow and brown—
with a peacock feather,
add them to white
and mix three together.
Sweeten with nectar
from hundreds of flowers.
Then heat until thick,
which needn't take hours.
Stir twice, then swallow
a spoonful or three.
A few words in Latin,
and the prince shall be free."*

"And the prince shall be free...," said Wales. "That has a nice ring to it. May we begin?"

They went directly to Sara's house. *"Add white to pink...,"* Wales said. "The white could be paint."

"Not if you're going to swallow it," Sara said. "I think the white will have to be milk."

"Then the something pink could be a pink bowl, like the one on the table," Wales said.

"All right," Sara agreed, pouring milk into the pink bowl. "Now, what about yellow?"

Bananas didn't seem right and neither did lemons.

Just then a chicken squawked. "Eggs!" Wales yelled.
Sara put a couple of eggs on the table.

Finding something suitable and brown was harder.
Sara went through the kitchen cupboards three times.
Then she thought of spices. "A dash of nutmeg?" she asked.

"That sounds good," said Wales. "Now . . . *yellow and brown—with a peacock feather, add them to white and mix three together.*"

Sara happened to have three peacock feathers, bought at a fair the summer before.

She put the egg yolks into the pink bowl and sprinkled some nutmeg on top. Wales stirred everything together with one of the feathers.

Sara continued, "*Sweeten with nectar from hundreds of flowers. Wildflower Honey,*" said Sara. "One cup or two?"

"One cup should be enough," Wales answered.

Sara poured the mixture into a pan on the stove. "*Heat until thick.*" (Which didn't take hours.) "*Stir twice, then swallow a spoonful or three.*"

"It's pudding!" Wales exclaimed. "Pudding isn't very magical." He sounded upset.

"Now," Sara said, "we need *a few words in Latin.*"

Wales thought hard. "Presto chango? No. Hocus-pocus. No, that's not right. HOLUS BOLUS!" he shouted.

Would it work? The words probably weren't Latin. The magic potion was only pudding. And the spell was for toads, not for donkeys.

But Wales was changing after all.

Gone were the long ears, the tail, and the four hoofs. In their place were . . . long ears . . . a tail . . . and four paws.

"It worked!" Wales cried.

"But you're a dog," Sara said.

Wales hung his head. "I used to live next door to a magician. He got tired of my chasing his cat, so he changed me into a donkey. No one would help me when I said I was an enchanted dog. Finally I decided to say that I was really a handsome prince. And you *did* help me," he finished.

"I would have helped you anyway," Sara replied.

In truth, she was somewhat relieved. The usual thing when one helps a handsome prince is to go with him to a palace in a faraway kingdom. Sara liked her house and her garden and her days at the market. She wasn't sure she was ready for a handsome prince in her life.

But a dog named Wales was a different matter.

26

It's All in Your Head

By Marilyn Burns

Sara helped Wales solve his problem. My imagination helps me solve problems too. I see how things are, and my imagination helps me see how they might be. My imagination improves with exercise, but it needs different exercises than the ones for my body. They help sharpen my senses. I try to imagine:

☐ the taste of peanuts.

☐ the smell of petrol.

☐ the sound of a car starting.

☐ the feel of swinging high on a swing.

Can you imagine them? Rate yourself on each one.

Why is this important? Remember, someone invented pizza. There wasn't always soft fabric for pyjamas. Whoever invented these things did more than just look.

Use your "stretched" senses to see if you can find a link between the following groups of words. What do they have in common?

pencil	apple	football
flower	lamp	lemon
basket	stapler	day

It's fun to try these with a friend. There are no right answers. But this kind of thinking can come in handy when you are faced with a problem. Any connection could be the leading clue. . . .

When horses pulled wagons in cities, they often wore blinkers over their eyes. They kept the horses from seeing anything except what was directly in front of them. That way they wouldn't get scared and upset the apple cart. Blinkers don't work so well for people. If I take off my mental blinkers, I can usually solve a problem. I have to look all around it sometimes, rather than right at it.

I bet you won't solve these two problems if you keep your blinkers on! Arrange ten coins like this:

You can move only three coins. Make the arrangement point in the opposite direction.

One way to begin: start moving coins. That's the Plunge-Right-In method. Not bad if it works.

But look at it backwards. You already know where you have to end up. What's the same about both arrangements? What's different?

(Hint: This drawing helps you see which to move.)

For the next problem you need six glasses, three empty and three full of water. Line them up like this:

Touch or move only one glass. Change the line so no empty is next to an empty, and no full is next to a full.

It may help to get six more glasses. Arrange them as they should be at the end of the problem. Can you see now which glass to move?

(Hint: No one said pouring was illegal.)

Sometimes I try stretching my imagination by looking at something I know well in a different way.

For example, in two minutes:

☐ List all the uses that could be made of an empty tin can.
☐ List ways that you could earn money.
☐ List all the things you could do to improve where you live.

The more your imagination stretches, the more you can use it, have fun with it, and create with it.

First Adventures

Tell me
What's new dear?
What's
New with you dear?
Where
Will you go next?
What
Will you do?

By Karla Kuskin

The Gift

By Ragnhildur Guttormsson
Illustrated by Tina Holdcroft

It is 1811. Ian McDuff and his father are sailing to Canada from Scotland with a group of settlers. Canada is a young country, and they want to help open up Manitoba for future settlers. They are just sighting their new country for the first time.

One morning when Ian and his friend came out, a deck-hand shouted at them, "Take a look at your new country!" They did, and saw a rocky black coast, streaked with white. "Like it?" he asked. "Yes!" they both shouted.

This was Labrador, and they still had a long way to go. But at last, after a journey of two months, they dropped anchor at York Factory.

On the *Edward and Ann* all was bustle and confusion. Those who were able were bringing their luggage. Others assisted the sick people on deck. The sailors were busy, hauling down and stowing the sails. Ian stood by the railing, looking towards the shore of Rupertsland. It was snow-covered and a fringe of ice had formed at the beach. But in the background there was a jagged edging of green, an evergreen forest.

His father, Angus, and Murray joined him at the railing.

"Ah, it's good to see land again," said Murray. "I've had enough of the sea." He leaned against the railing.

"What heaven-sent fragrance! I could swear it was the smell of Scotch fir," he said as he took a long breath.

"Yes, sir, it smells like Scotland," shouted Ian.

"That's a good beginning," decided Angus, smiling. The shore looked cold, unfriendly and lonely but it was land, after two months on the rolling ocean.

Soon Ian was on the sloop that had come to meet the ship. The wind filled the sail and the shore came rushing to meet him. It felt strange and awkward to walk on a firm pier after weeks on the swaying deck. At the end of the pier he stepped on an icy stone and fell flat on his face.

"Right smack into the arms of Rupertsland!" said one of the men as he picked him up. "Just like William the Conqueror when he landed in England."

There was nowhere for the colonists to stay at York Factory, so they had to build their own winter quarters. Macdonell chose the site for these at the bottom of a hill, sheltered by a forest of white spruce.

"Lots of good moss here," Kinlay said. "We'll need to fill in the cracks between the logs."

"That's your job, Ian. You'll gather the moss."

Before the winter set in, the huts were all ready and

large piles of firewood had been stacked at every hut. Ian took great pride in the fact that he had gathered all the moss used to fill the cracks between the logs.

Then it was Christmas Eve. In Ian's hut the supper was just over. A hunk of the unpleasant salted deer meat was still left on the table. There was an explosive sound from Kinlay. "Pshaw! Christmas! Salted meat and one tallow candle!" He threw on his buckskin jacket and shot out of the door. The cold rushed in, and a cloud of steam hung in the air.

Before long the door creaked and Kinlay's face showed in the opening. "Come, you fellows, and see." His voice sounded urgent. They all went to the door.

Never had Ian seen anything so gloriously beautiful! The whole sky was a mass of wavering sheets of light. Swiftly changing colours of gold, green and red played before their eyes like a living flame. Ian stared, fascinated. The beams of light seemed to be reaching for him and he thought he heard strange whispering sounds. Awe held him and he pressed closer to his father.

The cold soon drove them in. How dark the hut was! But the lone candle shone out, bringing comfort.

General Store

By Rachel Field
Illustrated by June Lawrason

Some day I'm going to have a store
With a tinkly bell hung over the door,
With real glass cases, and counters wide,
And drawers all spilly with things inside.

There'll be a little of everything;
Bolts of calico; balls of string;
Jars of peppermint; tins of tea;
Pots and kettles and crockery;
Seeds in packets; scissors bright;
Kegs of sugar, brown and white;
Sarsaparilla for picnic lunches;
Bananas and rubber boots in bunches.

I'll fix the window and dust each shelf,
And take the money in all myself.
It will be my store, and I will say,
"What can I do for you today?"

A Long School Day

By Bobbie Kalman
Illustrated by Barbara Reid

*When children went to school long ago, their school day was
very different from yours.*

Peter and Dorothy attend a one-room country school.
It is eight o'clock on a cold, winter morning and they are
starting on their hour-long walk to school. They have
been awake for hours. Dorothy has been churning butter
and Peter has been helping Father mend a fence.

They set off with their home-made copybooks and
hand-me-down readers. This year Dorothy is quite proud
because she has her very own feather quill and ink bottle.
Peter is a little jealous. He still has to use a slate and chalk.

Opening exercises

Dorothy and Peter arrive just in time for the opening exercises. The bell rings and the class marches in single file into the school and into their seats. Mr. Plunkett, the teacher, reads from the Bible and then the class recites a prayer. The teacher tells the students when to stand and kneel by ringing the bell on his desk. The first bell means "get ready". When the second bell rings, everyone stands. Bell three means everyone must step into the aisles. And when the fourth bell rings—get down on your knees!

Next Mr. Plunkett reads the roll call. Daniel Brown is missing again and Mr. Plunkett always locks out late comers. Late pupils are allowed in after break.

Reading and writing

The first class is reading and writing. The students are divided into four groups of two grades each. Each group has a reader. Peter is in his third year and second reader. While Mr. Plunkett listens to the young ones recite the alphabet forwards and backwards (and then backwards without looking!), the older pupils copy from their readers. Their handwriting is beautiful! Then the higher grades recite while the lower grades copy their letters.

Geography

Geography class is at ten o'clock. The pupils have to memorize the names of countries, lakes, rivers, and mountains. They use a big globe on a stand which Mr. Plunkett twirls so fast that all the colours run together.

Break

After geography there is a ten-minute break. By the time the pupils put on all their winter clothes, they have only a few minutes outside. On the way in they are allowed to take a drink from the bucket of water by the door. Today it is Peter's turn to bring in firewood for the stove.

Arithmetic

Arithmetic is next. Each class works out problems on slates. Afterwards the classes are drilled—they have to add, subtract, multiply, and divide out loud without writing anything down. No one volunteers. When pupils raise their hands, they had better be very sure they can answer quickly and correctly. Mr. Plunkett gives no points for just trying—the pupils have to succeed.

Spelling and grammar

After eating lunch, which the children bring with them, it is time for grammar. Grammar lessons begin as soon as the children learn to read, and continue until they leave school. Hardly anybody likes grammar. Some even prefer spelling! The younger pupils spell aloud words written on the blackboard. The older ones have drills. They scribble furiously to keep up with Mr. Plunkett, who delights in racing his students. Every Friday afternoon the school holds a spelling match. Believe it or not, it is the most exciting part of the week!

Class dismissed!

Classes finally end. "School, attention!" barks Mr. Plunkett. But no one can go home yet. Now comes Mr. Plunkett's business meeting. "Mary O'Brien," he says, "you will stay late for speaking in class. Jack Johnson, you will stay and clean the class-room to make up for misbehaving. Daniel Brown, you will be responsible for lighting the stove every morning for the next month in order to cure your lateness. Be here before all the other pupils, and see you're not the cause of them freezing to death. And you, Arthur Black, will be whipped the next time I hear of you fighting on the way home from school. The rest of you, go home without delay and make your manners to your parents." (Making one's manners means bowing for the boys and curtsying for the girls.)

"Arrange your desks," continues Mr. Plunkett. The pupils hurriedly tidy their books and slates.

"Ready!" calls Mr. Plunkett. All is completely quiet.

"Rise!" Everyone rises at once.

"March! One, two, three, four; one, two, three..."

At five o'clock Peter and Dorothy arrive home, eat supper, and are soon put to work helping Mother and Father with chores.

Canada Is My Home

By Garry Son Hoan

Nine-year-old Garry Son Hoan is one of Canada's recent immigrants from Vietnam. Garry had to leave his country without his parents. He has not seen them since the night he left them on the seashore in Vietnam. But he has thought about them a lot. He wanted to share some of his new experiences with his mother. His letters tell us a lot about Canada, too.

Dear Mother,

I took my first trip to the market the other day. To get there we took a train called the streetcar. They drive right down the middle of the streets on tracks. All the cars must drive around them. I have never seen so many cars in my whole life as I see each day in this city. They are always fighting with the streetcars, and there is hardly room for everything on the roads all at one time. We take the buses and trains everywhere now. We never walk—it is much too cold. Everyone says Canada is not like this all the time, but it has not been warm once since we got here. Last night was so cold that snow fell. This is white stuff that falls out of the sky like rain. Snow makes more bother because we have to wear more clothes. There are large rubber shoes we wear to keep our feet dry. (I remember in Saigon we could walk without shoes all year long.)

In the market here there are huge electric ice-boxes, the word for them is refrigerator. People have them in their own houses. We do, too. I don't know why. It is so cold you could leave things outside, but maybe animals would get them. All the food here comes in boxes or paper or plastic. Here they even put *milk* in boxes! All our vegetables are put in plastic bags, then into big boxes. Everything is bright-coloured and pretty, but I can't tell what's inside. When you want to pay for your food, you have to line up in front of a machine—you line up for almost everything here. At the machine they find out how much money you pay.

At the markets you never see anything alive. Many things come hard and cold and dead. This is called frozen—something they do in the ice-boxes. The chickens come in plastic packages with no heads or feathers or feet. You hardly know it's a chicken. It even tastes different. I remember how they used to kill and wash the chickens at home. I miss you.

Love,
Garry

Dear Mother,

Today, finally, was the first day of school. I went for the first time this morning. It was fun. We have a big new school building. It is so nice it is hard to believe it is just a school. I will go each morning at half past eight for five days and then not for two days. I am not alone at school. There are many others here learning English.

I understand much of what the teacher says. He is very nice. There is no Chinese or Vietnamese. Everything is in English. I guess we will start learning to read and write soon. This may be harder than talking. It looks so funny.

I will send you some of my English work next time.

Love,
Garry

Dear Mother,

Sometimes after school the teachers take us for some fun called skating. For me, at first, it was mostly falling. There are ponds of ice—frozen water—all over Toronto. You wear funny shoes with knives on the bottom. This cuts the ice and lets you stand up . . . sometimes. It is very slippery and this is the fun. Soon you learn to slide on top of the ice and you can go very fast. Everybody skates in Canada, even the grown-up people, and they play a game called hockey. This is done with sticks and skates and I love it. I now like winter. There is lots of snow on the ground. It can be good fun, too. It rolls into balls that we all throw at each other.

I talk and read and write English every day now. The teachers say I am a clever cat. That means I am smart and understand English. It is not hard.

I forgot to say in my other letter that we have lunch at school, too. They do everything for us there. Yesterday they gave me bread and brown paste. It was made from peanuts! I almost choked. There are red and yellow pastes to put on everything, and one to wash your teeth with. They like these pastes.

I don't think my teacher knows how much I know already. Sometimes he talks to me like a baby. Yesterday he took me over to the wall and lifted the light switch and said, "E-lec-tri-ci-ty". Sometimes I wonder.

Love,
Garry

Dear Mother,

I thought Canada would always be cold, but warm weather is here. Spring has arrived. There are flowers everywhere. The sun and the colours are bright like the days I spent with you at the flower market in Saigon.

I am very happy, though I miss you and Daddy. In school they tell us that Canada is happy to have us here, and all the other foreigners, too. People who do not look the same or talk the same are welcome and Canadians give them gifts. It is so different from Vietnam and I don't understand this. I hope the bad things have stopped there. Now I speak English and I have learned to skate and play hockey. We have been very lucky, I know. I remember when I first came here I was afraid. I am never afraid now. Each thing I do not know turns out to be fun to learn.

But on a day like this I almost forget that I am special, that I have come here over the sea in an aeroplane. I feel good. Canada is mine now. Canada is my home.

Love,
Garry

A Winter Song

Photography by Sam Samsalone,
Hot Shots Stock Shots Inc.

Let us walk upon the snow
      one and two
      one and two
What lies down below?

Down below the footsteps lie
      one and two
      one and two
And more and more of snow.

And what lies down
Below the more
The more and more of snow?

The Very Last First

By Jan Andrews
Illustrated by Marilyn Mets

Eva Padlyat lives in a village on Ungava Bay in the north of Quebec, Canada. She's an Eskimo, and for as long as she can remember, she's known how to walk on the bottom of the sea. It's something the people of her village often do in winter, when they want mussels to eat. Today, though, something special is going to happen. Today, for the very first time, Eva will walk on the bottom of the sea alone.

Eva and her mother stand in their small, warm kitchen. They put on heavy parkas and go out. They pull their hoods close to protect their faces from the cold wind and the sting of whipped-up snow. It is January, one of the worst months in the long Ungava winter.

Eva and her mother walk through the village. Each pulls behind her a small sledge. On the sledges are a shovel, a long ice-chisel, and a pan for mussels. Snow lies white as far as the eye can see. There are no trees on the vast northern tundra. There are no main roads, either. The village is off and away by itself.

The street Eva and her mother are on takes them past the school and down to the sea-shore. They meet a few friends on the way and stop for a quick greeting. Then they go on to cross the snow-covered beach. They step out on the thick sea ice. They've come at just the right time. The tide has pulled back from the land and there won't

be any water near the shore. They can go under the ice and wander about on the sea-bed quite safely.

"Goodbye," Eva's mother says. "Be careful, and good luck."

Eva grins. "Good luck, yourself," she replies.

Eva plods on over bumps and ridges where the cold has frozen the waves. She looks toward the open sea, beyond the bay. She sees only ice and more ice, on and on. Finally Eva stops in what seems to be a good place, where the ice is raised and swollen. She shovels away a patch of snow. Then she works the sharp end of her chisel under a heaved-up crack in the ice to make a hole. It's hard work. The freeze-up came months ago and the ice is very thick.

When the hole is about one metre square, Eva lowers herself into the darkness. She stands in the under-ice cavern—proud and excited and alone. Eva lights a candle and its yellow light softens the blackness. The small light glistens on the ice shining over her head and on the wet, black stones and pools and seaweed at her feet.

Then, for a moment, she's afraid. It's too dark to see far. She knows it can be dangerous down here. The under-ice world stretches far across the bay. Out there the sea tide is already beginning to lap back. She'll have to be careful. If she forgets how long she's been down, the tide could catch her. If she goes too far, she could lose her way back. Eva shivers, then laughs to herself.

"I'd better get to work," she says.

Eva puts her candle between two stones and starts

collecting mussels. She has chosen her spot well. Wherever she turns, her candle shows up strings of blue-black mussel shells. Before long her pan is full.

Eva goes back to the ice hole. She sets her pan down and listens for the sound of the waves. The tide is still quite a way out. There's plenty of time to do what she has always wanted. Now she can enjoy being by herself down here in the dark, mysterious, undersea winter world.

Eva sings a tune, quietly at first, then loudly. The echoes of her singing bounce off the ice at her. She shouts to herself and is glad. She dances a little dance. She pokes in rock pools and makes strange shadows with her candle.

She lifts up seaweed in long, flat ribbon strands. Then she lets them down with a flop.

At last Eva hears a voice. Her mother is calling through the ice hole. "Are you all right down there? Are you nearly done?"

Eva takes her candle and goes back to the hole. She picks up her mussel pan. "Of course. I'm coming up now."

She climbs out into the fresh air and feels the cold wind on her face again.

"You've done well," her mother says. "You must have chosen a better place than I did."

They load up the sledges again and Eva takes her mother's hand. Together they walk over the ice. They cross the beach and go through the village. Already twilight has fallen. Daylight lasts a very few hours this far north in January.

Eva glances back over her shoulder at the mussel shells. She thinks of popping them in boiling water, watching them open, and tasting the salty shellfish.

"That's my last very first time," she says sadly. "My very last very first time for walking alone under the sea."

Eva's mother laughs. "You really like it down there, don't you?"

"Yes," Eva answers. She thinks of the black glistening ice and the faint humming of the tide far out to sea. She remembers being frightened when she first stood alone in the huge cavern. She remembers dancing on the sea floor once her mussel pan was full. "Yes I do."

The Tale

If you're a pretender, come sit by my fire
For we have some flax-golden tales to spin.
Come in!
Come in!

By Shel Silverstein

The Tale Spi

Spinners
Spinners
Spinners
pinners
pinners
ners

A Tale of the Hodja

By Barbara K. Walker
Illustrated by Greg Ruhl

In Turkey, several hundred years ago, there lived a certain Nasreddin Hodja. In his town in Turkey, the Hodja served as a judge in local disputes. But like the rest of us, the Hodja was only human. Sometimes when he tried to be very wise, he was foolish; and sometimes when he seemed to be foolish, he was in truth very wise. Above all, he was able to laugh at his own mistakes.

A great many tales have been written about the Hodja. Here is one for your delight.

The Woodcutter's Hunh-Sayer

One day as the Hodja was walking through the forest, he came upon a peasant cutting wood. It was hard, heavy work, and every blow of the axe took all the force the peasant could muster. As the Hodja watched, he heard someone saying "*Hunh!*" every time the axe came down. There on a log sat the woodcutter's companion. And faithfully with every blow he said, "Hunh!" The Hodja wondered at this, but went on his way without speaking.

In a few days, the peasant went to the bazaar with his load of wood and sold it for a fair sum in coins. As he slipped the sack of coins into the pocket of his baggy trousers, his companion rushed up. "Half of that money is mine!" he insisted. "I did half of the work."

Astonished, the woodcutter debated the matter. Clearly this was a case to be brought before the judge. Accordingly the two went before the Hodja, who served the village as judge. Carefully the Hodja listened to both sides of the case. Then, calling the woodcutter to him, he directed him to lay the bag of coins on a flat stone. One by one the Hodja dropped the coins on the stone. As they rang out with a pleasant jingle, he said to the companion, "Do you hear this?"

"Yes," the companion answered.

"Fine," said the Hodja. "The *sound* is yours and the *coin* is the woodcutter's."

When the coins had all been sounded and turned over to the woodcutter, the Hodja dismissed the case.

The Little Rooster's Diamond Penny

By Marina McDougall
Illustrated by Maureen Shaughnessy

Long ago there lived a poor woman who had a little rooster. He wasn't just an ordinary rooster, although his mistress did not know it. They both lived in an old tumbledown cottage by the roadside.

One day as the little rooster was pecking away in the yard, he found a shining diamond penny.

"What good luck," the little rooster thought. "Now my mistress can go and buy some food."

At that very moment, the Sultan came riding by with his army. His eyes filled with greed at the sight of the diamond penny.

"Guards," ordered the Sultan, "take the diamond penny from this rooster at once!"

The poor little rooster scratched the guards with his claws and pecked their hands with his beak, but they were too strong for him. They took the penny from him.

The little rooster was very angry. Instead of running away, he flew up and hid inside one of the guards' cloaks. Holding on very tightly, he managed to ride along with the guard all the way to the Sultan's palace. As soon as they arrived there, he sneaked out, flew to the top of the wall of the palace gardens and started to crow.

"Cock-a-doodle-doo, Sultan, give me back my diamond penny!"

The Sultan stomped into his palace and banged the window shut. But the little rooster perched on the window ledge and made a louder racket than before.

"Cock-a-doodle-doo, Sultan, give me back my diamond penny!"

This made the Sultan very angry. He wasn't used to anyone going against his wishes.

"Go!" he said to his servant. "Catch that rooster and drown him in the well!"

The servant caught the little rooster by the wings and threw him into the well. But as soon as the little rooster hit the water, he did a very strange thing. He began to murmur to himself very softly.

"Gizzard, gizzard, magic gizzard, suck in all this water!"

And sure enough, soon all the water was gone from the well.

Then the little rooster shook the water from his wings, flew up to the Sultan's window and started to crow again.

"Cock-a-doodle-doo, Sultan, give me back my diamond penny!"

The Sultan stamped his big foot, and his face turned purple with rage.

"Go!" he shouted to his servant. "Catch that rooster and roast him alive in the oven!"

This time the little rooster didn't put up a fight. He even smiled a little to himself as the big servant threw him into the flames. As soon as the oven door closed on him, he started his magical chant.

"Gizzard, gizzard, magic gizzard, let out all the water and put out the fire!"

In an instant, all the water came spurting from his bottomless gizzard and soon the fire was out.

Very pleased with himself, the little rooster flew out of the oven through the chimney. Once again he perched on the Sultan's window sill and crowed at the top of his lungs.

"Cock-a-doodle-doo, Sultan, give me back my diamond penny!"

The Sultan's next command to his servant was even more cruel.

"Go!" he yelled. "Catch that rooster and throw him into the beehive. The bees will sting him to death."

The obedient servant snatched the little rooster by his tail and flung him into the beehive. When the servant left, the little rooster began his secret chant.

"Gizzard, gizzard, magic gizzard, suck in all the bees!"

As before, the bees quickly disappeared down the little rooster's throat.

Delighted with his trick, the little rooster clattered up to the Sultan's window and began to crow and clamour.

"Cock-a-doodle-doo, Sultan, give me back my diamond penny!"

In his fury the Sultan tore at his black beard. Then a slow, wicked smile spread over his face.

"Go!" he ordered his servant. "Catch that little rooster and bring him back to me. I'll handle him myself. I'll put him inside my bloomers and sit on him."

The little rooster could hardly wait to get into those big bloomers. As soon as he was inside the Sultan's pants, he murmured to himself.

"Gizzard, gizzard, magic gizzard, let out all the bees to sting the Sultan's seat!"

"Ouch, ow, oh my seat!" cried the Sultan, jumping up and down. "Take that little rooster to my treasure house and let him have his penny back!"

The guards escorted the little rooster to the treasure house and waited for him to pick out his diamond penny. Quick as a wink, the little rooster spoke the magic words.

"Gizzard, gizzard, magic gizzard, suck in all this treasure!"

In the treasure house there were three tubs full of money and seven chests of precious stones. When his gizzard was filled with treasures, the little rooster turned towards home and half flew, half ran until he landed at his mistress's front door.

"Look what I've brought you!" he cried loudly. He let out all the treasures from his magic gizzard right in front of the house. The sparkling mound of riches was as high as a mountain beside the poor woman's house.

The little rooster and his mistress danced with joy around the treasure heap, for they knew they would never again go hungry.

Meet the Author

By Rivka Cranley
Photographed by Harold Whyte

You've just read the tale about the clever rooster. Now meet Marina McDougall who wrote the story.

Marina, where did you get the idea for the story, "The Little Rooster's Diamond Penny"?

It was my favourite bedtime story as a child. When I was young, an aunt and uncle lived with us. Aunt Irene would come in every night to ask me which story I wanted to hear. And every night I would ask for "The Little Rooster's Diamond Penny". This went on for three years!

I decided to write down this story when I had my own children. I wanted them to have a chance to enjoy folk tales from other countries. I also wanted them to find out something about their own Hungarian background.

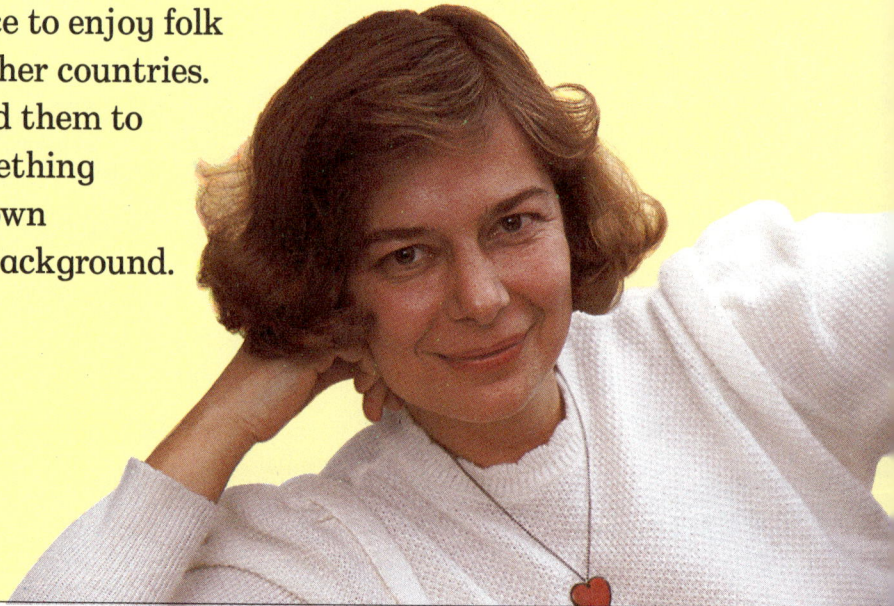

66

How do you come up with ideas for your other stories?

While I'm working on one story, I find a lot of other ideas popping into my head. And they always seem better and more wonderful than the one I'm working on. So I jot down these ideas quickly, and then I put them in a special place where I can go back to them after I've finished the story I'm working on. Right now my special place is a loose-leaf binder. You should see some of the incredible ideas that are just waiting to be made into stories!

What do you like best about writing stories for children?

I like to catch the spirit of the children I'm writing for. I try to picture in my mind who is going to be reading my story, and I think about them all the time while I do my writing. I believe writing is a skill that I know how to do. I do it for an audience to enjoy, and I get a great deal of pleasure knowing children will find my stories entertaining. Writing is not only fun, it's sort of a joy for me.

Why do you think children like your stories?

It's the funny, silly elements in the fantasy stories that children like. The more fantastic and the sillier the story, the better they like it. And a lot of my stories are taken from old folk tales. Anybody who writes folk tales is starting with a big advantage. You know these stories have survived for hundreds of years. That means only one thing. It was a good story from the beginning. If you

think of all the stories that are ever told, and only the very best are still around, you know you're already working with first-class material when you sit down to write a folk tale. If children liked "The Little Rooster's Diamond Penny" two hundred years ago, they'll still enjoy it today.

What kind of advice do you have for children who want to start writing stories?

To take an idea and make it into a real story, a lot of writing and rewriting has to take place. Most children will really enjoy that first part of writing down a really silly idea. That's what I call the raw material. It's like going down into a mine. You find a rock that's very valuable. There you have the raw material. But then you have to dig out the rock, clean it, shape it, maybe even polish it. You have to do the same thing when you write. That's the most important idea I would like to get across to all the would-be writers. Start with an idea, then work on it, clean it, shape it before you're done with it. I wrote and rewrote "The Little Rooster's Diamond Penny" quite a few times before I was happy with it. I remember one story that I had to rewrite fourteen times before it was good enough!

Writers have to remember one thing. A story grows and changes the more you work on it. And all that work will make the story better . . . so don't give up—keep writing!

The Raven, the Dove and the Whale

By Kimberly Buis, age nine
Illustrated by Marilyn Mets

A raven was sitting in a tree, wondering what to do.

All of a sudden a dove came along and asked, "Would you play hide-and-seek with me?"

The raven thought a moment and then said, "Yes." The raven closed his eyes and counted, "Caw, caw, caw." A few minutes later he found the dove's hiding spot.

Now it was the raven's turn. He was going to find the best place in the world to hide. The raven thought and thought before he finally said, "In a whale!" He flew over the wide blue sea until he spotted a sperm whale. "Ah, the perfect place," he said.

He dived for the whale's blow-hole. Pop—he was half-way in, but that wasn't enough. He twisted and turned, but he couldn't get in and he couldn't get out.

All of a sudden he felt something strange happening. Before he knew it, the raven was thrown up in the air on some water. Soon after, the dove found him and they flew back together.

Some people came across the whale one day and noticed that the blow-hole was shaped like an S. The raven, when he was twisting and turning, must have made it that way. And to this day the sperm whale's blow-hole is shaped like an S.

Journey Cake, Ho!

By Ruth Sawyer
Illustrated by Deborah Drew-Brook-Cormack

There were three of them: the old woman, Merry; the old man, Grumble; and Johnny, the farm-hand. They lived in a log cabin, t'other side of Tip Top Mountain.

The old woman took care of the wool; she carded and spun and knitted it. She laid the fire, tended the griddle, churned the butter, and sang at her work. The song she liked best ran thiswise:

"Ho, for a Journey Cake—
Quick on a griddle bake!
Sugar and salt it,
Turn it and brown it,
Johnny, come eat it with milk for your tea."

The old man tended the garden patch, sheared the sheep, milked the cow, felled the trees, sawed the logs, and grumbled at his work. The grumble he liked best was:

"A bother, a pest!
All work and no rest!
Come winter, come spring,
Life's a nettlesome thing."

And what about Johnny? He split the kindling, filled the woodbox, lugged the water, fed the creatures, fished the brook, and whistled at his work. One tune was as fine as another to Johnny.

Their whole world lay close about them. There were the garden patch, the brook, the logging road that ran down to the valley where the villagers lived, and the spruce woods.

On the tallest tree sat Raucus, the sentinel crow, watching and waiting to caw when surprise or trouble was near.

Nothing happened for a long, long time. They lived snug, like rabbits in their burrow. Then—

One night a fox carried off the hens. "Caw, caw!" called the crow. But it was too late. The next night a wolf carried off the sheep. "Caw, caw, caw!" called the crow. But it was too late.

There came a day when the pig wandered off and got himself lost. Last of all the cow fell into the brook and broke her leg.

All that day the crow cawed and cawed and cawed.

That night the old woman said, shaking her head, "Trouble has come. The meal chest is low, the bin is near empty. What will feed two will not feed three."

The old man grumbled and said, "Johnny, 'tis likely you'll be leaving us on the morrow and finding yourself a new master and a new ma'am."

The next morning by sun-up, the old woman had run together a piece of sacking and put straps to it to hold Johnny's belongings—a knife, some gum from the spruce trees, his shoes, and a washing-cloth. On top went the Journey Cake that had been baked for him. It was large, round, and crusty-hard. "Now be off with you!" said the old man, grumbling. "What must be, must be."

"Off with you—and luck follow after," said the old woman sadly.

Johnny said nothing at all. He left his whistle behind him and took the logging road down to the valley.

Right foot, left foot, right foot, left foot. He was half-way down and more when the straps on his sacking bag broke loose. Out bounced the Journey Cake.

It bumped and it bumped; it rolled over and over. Down the road it went, and how it hollered!

"Journey Cake, ho!
Journey Cake, hi!
Catch me and eat me
As I roll by!"

Away and away rolled the Journey Cake. Away and away ran Johnny.

Faster and faster. They passed a field full of cows. A brindle cow tossed her head and took after them. She mooed:

"At running I'll beat you.
I'll catch you and eat you!"

Faster and faster, faster and faster! They passed a pond full of ducks.

"Journey Cake, ho!
Journey Cake, hi!
Catch me and eat me
As I roll by!"

A white duck spread her wings and away and away she went after them, quacking:

"At flying I'll beat you.
I'll catch and I'll eat you!"

Faster and faster, faster and faster! They came to a meadow where sheep were grazing. A white sheep and a black sheep took after them.

Now they were through the valley and the road began to climb. Slower and slower rolled the Journey Cake. Slower and slower ran Johnny, the brindle cow, the white duck, and the two sheep.

"Journey Cake, hi!

The journey is long.

Catch me and eat me

As I roll along."

They passed a wallow. A spotted pig heard them and came a-grunting.

They passed a barnyard and a flock of red hens flew over the stump fence, squawking. Slower and s-l-o-w-e-r, higher and higher.

At last they came to a mountain pasture where a grey

donkey was feeding. Now the Journey Cake was huffing and puffing:

"Journey Cake, hi!
The journey is long.
C-c-catch me and eat me—
As I roll along."

The donkey was fresh. He kicked up his heels and brayed:

"I'll show I can beat you.
I'll catch you and eat you."

Higher went the road. Slower and slower, slower and slower rolled the Journey Cake—t'other side of Tip Top Mountain. Slower and slower and slower, slower and slower came the procession with Johnny at the head. Huffing and puffing, they circled the spruce woods. From his perch on the tallest tree, Raucus the crow let out his surprise warning: "Caw, caw, caw!"

Johnny heard it. He stopped all of a quickness. There was the brook; there was the garden patch; there was the log cabin.

He was home again. The Journey Cake had brought him to the end of his journey!

The Journey Cake spun around twice and fell flat. "I'm all of a tucker!" it hollered.

"We're all of a tucker," cried the others. The red hens found a house waiting for them. The cow found her tether rope; the pig found a sty; the duck found a brook; the sheep found a place for grazing; and the donkey walked himself into the shed.

The old woman came a-running.

The old man came a-running.

Johnny hugged them hard. He found his whistle again and took up the merriest tune. "Wheee—ew, wheee—ew!" he whistled. He hopped first on right foot, then on left foot. When he had his breath, he said, "Journey Cake did it. Journey Cake fetched me-and-the-cow-and-the-white-duck-and-the-black-and-white-sheep-and-the-flock-of-red-hens-and-the-pig-and-the-grey-donkey. Now they are all yours!"

The old man forgot his best grumble. The old woman picked up the Journey Cake and went inside to freshen it up on the griddle. She went, singing the song she liked best:

"Warm up the Journey Cake;
From now on it's Johnny Cake.
Johnny, come eat it
With milk for your tea!"